WHITE COLLAR CRIMES-TRICK TO BE COME WEALTHY

VOLUME 2, ISSUE 1 OF BRILLOPEDIA

KAARKUZHALI EKAMBARAM

Contents

Preface

"Start writing, no matter what. The water does not flow until the faucet is turned on".

-Louis L'Amour

Hundreds of students and professors are contributing their work to Brillopedia, we are here to provide ample information about Law and Contemporary issues. Our aim is to provide a platform for today's generation to express their views and ideas on law and contemporary law.

Publication

This research paper is published in volume 2, issue 1 of Brillopedia

Author

CHAPTER ONE

ABSTRACT

This research article analyzes the most crucial crime passing in the country which is the white collar crimes and how it affects the country's economy and its impact on the society. White collar crimes are a big global concern and are increasing at an terrified rate because it results in the country's underdevelopment. It can also be called as the crime of educated and professional elites. The people who are committing this crime have usually a better understanding of technology, their respective field, disciplines etc. They maintain their respect in the society until the crime is discovered.These crimes are committed on large and small scales everyday. These crimes bear immediate intervention by the government by not only making strict laws but also ensuring its proper implementation. When a white collar crime is committed huge losses on business occur which have a direct impact on the consumers and the society. There are various numbers of frauds and scams that have been exposed in our country from the past few years like 2g scam,banking scam, and many more. Due to these frauds the economy of our country has affected. There is loss in every field from the costs of commodities to the securities and insurance. Let's discuss why this white collar crime arises and how it affects society. Further, it deals with variations among different crimes and also the types of white collar crimes.This paper highlights various legislations of Indian laws which talks about the punishment of these types of crimes. The author will finally conclude the article with his own suggestions. Eventually, how to annihilate these crimes from the country for its development.

__KEYWORDS :-__White collar crimes, Blue collar crimes, victimless, Biggest scam, legislations, Eradication of root cause.

CHAPTER TWO

INTRODUCTION

As the society develops and the crimes in the society also increases. The crime profile haschanged a lot in recent times. The traditional crimes have been changed into white collarcrimes in the country. White collar crimes have become fashion currently. These are the mostnotorious crimes. This type of crimes are committed by the most reputed people in the societyand it also affects the society at large. These crimes are non violent crimes and victimless, their motive is generally fiscal in nature. These crimes are common in education, trade andcommerce and health etc. These crimes are done in a veritably systematic manner. They maintain their character in society. Generally a largely privileged section of people get involved in this type of crime. Let us look deep into this content.

LITERAL BACKGROUND

India is a developing country and white-collar crimes are the major cause for its under development. This white-collar crime leads to the loss of profitabl development of the country. Corruption, fraud and bribery are some of the most common white collar crimes in India. Once 10 timesthe rate of the white collar crimes are added.

DESCRIPTION

For the first time the term white-collar crime is defined by Edwin hard in - as" *crime scommitted by people who enjoy the high social status, great character and respectability in their occupation during the course of his employment*". These are non-violent crimes committed by businessmen and government professionals. It has a large impact on society. It's a socio profitable crime which affects society at large.

CHAPTER THREE

CAUSES OF WHITE COLLAR CRIMES

- Greed

Machiavelli said that a man can sooner and fluently forget the death of his father than of hisheritage. The same as applicable in the case of commission of white collar crimes because aman of high social status who's financially secure why he has to commit similar crimes if notoutof rapacity.!?

- Lack of mindfulness

The nature of white collar crimes are different from the traditional crimes. Most of thepeople weren't apprehensive of it and they fail to understand that they're the victims of thesecrimes

- Necessity

And the most important cause for the white collar crimes is the necessity. people commitwhite collar crimes to meet their own requirements and the requirements of their family but the most important thing that the people of high social status are doing these kinds of crimesis to satisfy and feed their ego and pride.

- Easy way to commit

The rapid-fire advancement in technology and business brought this new kind of culprits for committing similar white collar crimes. Technology has also made way to commit these crimes and to be get loss to the person because it provides the easy way of access to theprivate information of a person and the cost of similar crimes is much further than other crimes like murder, theft or burglary and so that the victim would take time to recover from it.

- Lack of strict laws

Also this kind of crimes are done through the internet and the digital styles of transferpayments the law seems to be not strict to pursue these cases because probing and tracking of these crimes becomes delicate and a complicated one. It becomes delicate because they're generally committed in the sequestration of a home or office there by furnishing no eye witnesses for these kinds of crimes.

CHAPTER FOUR

TYPES OF WHITE COLLAR CRIME

- Bank fraud

Bank fraud is a fraud committed on the banks it affects the public at large because there's arelation of trust between the banks and the public it's committed by the fraudulent companies by making false representations and it's also related to the manipulation of negotiable instruments like cheque bouncing, securities, Bank deposits etc. It affects the public as well as the Government of the country and it's the most common type of white collar crime. it's also known as a commercial crime.

- Cybercrime

Cyber crimes are crimes which are related to computer networks. It's the biggest cause forthe white collar crimes because that technology gets fleetly advanced and the crime related tothe technology also increases as well. These types of crimes are made directly or laterallyagainst the victim to cause damage to his character or to harm him mentally or physically bywayof using internet networks and other technological sources. This cybercrime threatensthe nation as well as the person's security and fiscal status. These crimes can beget huge loss to the person and also threatens the sequestration of the person because telling the non public information can produce problems. Also the cyber crimes against women are a fleet by way of using mobile phones, cyber stalking, transferring and filming women. Some exemplifications are Hacking, child pornography, brand violation, cyber terrorism.

- Bribery

It's the most common type of white collar crime. Bribery simply means giving a plutocrat or some goods to that person who's inauthority for the purpose of averring him to do acommodity or precluding him from doing the commodity. Also bribery has become the most common in come of thepublic officers ofour country.

- Money laundering

In money laundering, culprits try to hide the original power of the plutocrat and the placewhere they obtained that money by illegal means. To say simply it means to show the illegalmoneyas a licit money.

- Duty elusion

It means concealment of income which is done to reduce the liability of duty in the eyes ofthe government.

- Identity theft

In this crime they actually pierce the particular information of anyone similar as name, address, phone number etc. and use it to gain money.

CHAPTER FIVE

EFFECTS OF THE WHITE COLLAR CRIMES

- Effects on the Companies

In companies the white collar crimes lead to huge losses because when these crimes arecommitted in companies the company would raise the price of the product which leads to deduction of guests for the product. Since the company is in loss occasionally the hires for the workers will be reduced and some employment of the hand will be stopped or cut down which creates severance to that person and most importantly the investors of the company and its workers will find it difficult to repay their loans. In simple it works as per the law of demand which says that when the price of the commodity rises its demand would fall andwhenthe price lowers its demand would increase.

- Effect on Society

The white collar crimes produce a major impact in the society because the one who has toplay the responsible part in the society who sets an illustration is the one who's committingthe crime.

- Effect on Workers

This kind of crime creates a fear among the workers that they start distrusting if they're safeandthat they can still betrusted by the company.

<u>DIFFERENCE BETWEEN THE WHITE COLLAR CRIMES AND BLUE COLLAR CRIMES</u>

1. The term Blue collar crime came into actuality eventually in the 1920 the term wasused to relate to Americans who performed homemade labour they frequently favored cloths of darker shade so as to stains less visible some used to wear clothes with theblue- collar this worked for a low weight on an hourly base.
2. White collar crimes have been current since centuries and it isn't new to all types of businesses professions and diligence.
3. The difference between Blue collar crimes which are crimes of general nature andwhite collar crime which was financial and pre-planned nature.

The supreme court of India in the case of *state of Gujarat vs Mohanlal jitamalji porwalanr.* In this case it was said that one person can murder another person in the heat of the moment but causing fiscal loss or committing profitable offences requires planning.It involves computations and strategy making in order to get particular gains. These arethe characteristics of white collar crimes which can be distinguished from other kinds ofgeneralnature.

CHAPTER SIX

WHITE COLLAR CRIMES IN PROFESSIONS

- Legal

Hanging the substantiations of the other party, fabrication of the forged documents, violation of the ethics of the legal profession in orderto gain money.

- Education

Collecting further money in the name of donations from the scholars in order to giveadmission, donations rather of merit grounded admission, collecting huge amounts in the name of government subsidies.

- Health

Making false medical instruments by the croakers, dragging the case's treatment and faking in order to increase the bills, dealing sample drugs which aren't allowed to the druggists, exposing the gender of the child which is in the mother's womb for a bribe.

One example of India's biggest scam was *Harshad Mehta bank fraud.*

"Behind every great fortune lies a great crime".

He was a stockbroker and reputed in the stock market so the investors followed him blindly. He started his own brokerage firm "grow more". He used to choose the company which is not much valued and he increased the value of the share market of that company by selling shares. This was the 1st scam done by him. The second scam was that he took a loan of a huge amount from the bank without any security and purchased the shares at high prices thereby creating a false market. He misused his status and manipulated the stock prices for his gain. It resulted in unnatural pumping of money in stock markets causing an abnormal rise in the price of shares. Later, the RBI got involved in this issue and found out about this biggest scam.

<u>LEGISLATION FOR WHITE COLLAR CRIMES</u>

There are colorful legislations made by the government for preventingwhite collar crimes similar as

1. Indian penal code 1860
2. Income tax act 1961
3. Prevention of corruption act 1988
4. Prevention of money laundering act 2002
5. Commodities act 1955
6. Companies act 1960
7. IT act 2005

CHAPTER SEVEN

REPORTS ON WHITE COLLAR CRIMES

Numerous panels were formed to look into the white collar crimes and set up rules and regulations according to the inflexibility of the crimes and to help them and to exclude them.

- The report on the commission on the forestallment of corruption 1964-Central vigilance commission created in 1964 to address corruption in the government services and to cover all alerts under the central government.
- The report on the commission of enquiry on the administration of Dalmiajain companies 1963
- Administrative reforms commission on reports

MEASURES TO CURB WHITE COLLAR CRIMES

- There should be strict laws to help eradicate this kind of crime.
- Public mindfulness should be created about the white collar crimes because most of the public weren't aware of it.
- Government shouldn't neglect these crimes just because of not having victims, it should be taken reasonable care in order to help the frugality of the country.
- *"The punishment should fit the crime"* so the punishment should be made harder and stricter.
- The media has a key role to play in reducing the rate of increasing white collar crimes. It has been noted that most of the white collar crimes go unreported. So, if the media becomes more active towards publishing frauds and scams at higher levels and revealing how do the people at

higher position in a company use their powers arbitrarily, and also make efforts in making people aware about the white collar crimes, and avoid corrupt practices, then this would definitely help in reducing the rate at which the white collar crimes are being committed.

CHAPTER EIGHT

CONCLUSION

The white collar crimes produce a great impact on the frugality of the country and it leads the country as a whole. It harms the country by profitable fraud and the elimination of the levies. It not only affects the country but also it affects the people of the country and it creates a negative impact on the society. As people weren't apprehensive of this kind of crime, it's easier for those who are committing the crime.

"To prevent the country's economy from the scam; eradicate the root cause of the crimes."